THE ZEBRA STOOD IN THE NIGHT

Kerry Hardie was born in 1951 and grew up in County Down. She now lives in County Kilkenny with her husband, the writer Seán Hardie. Her poems have won many prizes, including the Michael Hartnett Award for Poetry in 2005. Her poems have featured in seven Bloodaxe anthologies: *Staying Alive, Being Alive, Being Human, Essential Poems from the* Staying Alive *Trilogy, The Poetry Cure, The New Irish Poets* and *Modern Women Poets.*

She has published six collections with the Gallery Press in Ireland: *A Furious Place* (1996), *Cry for the Hot Belly* (2000), *The Sky Didn't Fall* (2003), *The Silence Came Close* (2006), *Only This Room* (2009) and *The Ash and the Oak and the Wild Cherry Tree* (2012). Her *Selected Poems* (2011) was published by the Gallery Press in Ireland and by Bloodaxe Books in Britain. Her seventh collection, *The Zebra Stood in the Night*, was published by Bloodaxe Books in 2014. Her first novel, *Hannie Bennet's Winter Marriage* appeared in 2000; her second, *The Bird Woman* was published in 2006.

Kerry Hardie is a member of Aosdána.

KERRY HARDIE

The Zebra Stood in the Night

BLODAXE BOOKS

ISBN: 978 1 78037 111 5

First published 2014 by
Bloodaxe Books Ltd,
Eastburn,
South Park,
Hexham,
Northumberland NE46 1BS.

www.bloodaxebooks.com
For further information about Bloodaxe titles
please visit our website or write to
the above address for a catalogue.

Supported using public funding by

**ARTS COUNCIL
ENGLAND**

Cover design: Neil Astley & Pamela Robertson-Pearce.

Printed in Great Britain by Bell & Bain Limited, Glasgow, Scotland, on
acid-free paper sourced from mills with FSC chain of custody certification.

for Séan

ACKNOWLEDGEMENTS

Acknowledgements are due to the editors of the following journals in which some of these poems have appeared: *Archipelago, The Atlanta Review, Irish Pages, The Irish Times, Lines of Vision, The Manchester Review, The Missouri Review, Moth, Music and Literature, New Hibernia Review, Ploughshares, Poetry Ireland, Poetry London, Postcard Poems, The Salzburg Review, The Stinging Fly, Southword, Southword Journal Online, The Stony Thursday Book, Tiveret, The Ulster Tatler* and *The Yellow Nib.*

The author wishes to thank Kilkenny County Council for a residency at the Tyrone Guthrie Centre at Annaghmakerrig, Mayo County Council for a residency at the Heinrich Böll Cottage, Achill Island, and the Arts Council for the assistance of the Cnuas.

CONTENTS

PART ONE

Conditioning

It's all the stuff they taught us in our childhoods,
the lessons hammered from their smelt of pain –

insure, secure, and burglar-proof your cell,
equip with all the smartest apps and trends.

The future waits out there, pitch-black, unknown,
beyond the knife-edge of the precinct lights.

The zebra stood in the night

now it keeps flashing up on the screen of my mind,
the lines on its body sharp and precise,
no blurring of edges, no shading.
I'm surprised that I seem so surprised
at the hardship that's dwelling inside me.
Black, white, black, white.
No compromise. No bleed.

Musician

(for Maya Homburger)

There's something in the presence, in the carriage,
a dignity that makes the player disappear,
as though a lamp's been trimmed and lit and lifted,
a clear glass funnel placed around the flame –

The sound runs through the body, lifting clear,
so that I fly upon those sweet, high tones,
sounds that belong – not here – but somewhere else,
some other level that we partly dwell on,

as though the listening is given from there,
and we are being bowed like violins,
and when it's done, exhausted, we fall back
into the dailiness that lets us have our home.

Leaf-fall

(for Séan)

'Chestnuts are the stubbornest.'
The pithy brown husks
that shielded the fruits
lie scattered about on the grass.
Also leaves.
But so many still on the trees.

'It takes a frost.
Don't you remember?'

Yes, he remembers.
The first bitter night
and the leaves all unhook.
They drift in the stillness,
they settle like moths on the grass.

He likes these hidden patterns and decisions:
trees, opening their hands in the night,
letting fall
what they have no more use for;
likes cycles, secrets, metaphysics.
'Sound,' he said
'is the least of music – '
And flourishes of trumpets
furiously blew,
their voices streaming
silently
onto the air.

Sealed Vessel

It is hard not to hate
glutinous black slugs,

hard to include them
in life when they mostly appear

to be eating it. This winter has been so wet
the world teems with them. The snowdrops open,

the clean white lines of their petals eaten down
to a border of botched lacework.

Maybe they are
earth's lead, the alchemist's base metal –

poisonous, deadweight. Yet somehow
essential.

Magnolias

(for Ann Thornely 1939–2013)

Magnolias are making flame again,
white fire against the smoke-blue of the mountain.
Each year, the old, hard wood, the angles,
the pointed buds thrust up before the leaves.
Stroke of the sun, the closed pods burst,
the thick, white petals plunge and rear,
ecstatic in that rapturous disorder
that opens secret stamens to all comers –

Like life, like death, that does not know restraint,
but throws off flesh to strip the spirit naked,
hard with stored need, with lust for transformation,
to blast free from this mortal, knotted coil
and lift into the clean air of the mountain.

May Rain

It is May, and the rain is falling.
It's warm. Everything's swelling and drinking,
the birds have gone in, they cheep deep
in the walls of the white-thorn
that make of the garden a kingdom.

The whitethorn is flowering, it holds out its arms
to the rain. When the rain stops the perfume will rise,
a silence inside the green wall
that is splashed and dripping with blossom.
When the rain stops the birds will burst out,
will shout like the newly-arisen, up into the sky,
and the snails will go carrying their whorled shells about,
they'll vanish the shoots,
they'll pattern the new leaves with cut-work.

Me, too. I will come from the darkness
inside the green door, will walk the lost garden,
sniffing and touching,
sleeves wet, and the cuffs of my trousers,
hair wet from the pour of round drops
from the brushed-against leaves,
life wet from the green soak
of birdsong and roundness and rain.

Washing

is fluttering, bouncing, sails in the wind,
is dragging sad, an old dog's eyes,
is hanging us up to each other's gaze:
our two arms, two legs,
head, chest, arse, feet, the way we live,
and I bundle it up,
carry it in,
nose in its folds,
breathing wind and rain and lit weather.

Vacances

Marthe de Meligny speaks from the walls of the National Gallery, Dublin

It is nineteen twenty-three. We are blocking out the dead,
we are blocking in a world that's not at war.
There are pieces of light laid on bottles and glass,
a platter of fruits, my stretched arm.

Absence sits on the blue chair.
Everyone's holding their breath
waiting for what hasn't ended
to stand up and start up again.

Sunlight and fruit and white delph.
A striped dress, the spread of the cloth.
The darkness is held in the reach of my arms
right there, at the front of the scene,

at the front of this dance we're creating
to block out the Danse Macabre
that's rattling its bones from the trenches,
that's piling up armbands and flags.

Nobby of the Bogs

When we were home again
you got up from your place
in the reed-bed beside the river,
flopped up and across the empty trees –
I thought: I saw you last in London
when I happened to look up –
too heavy really for air, your nib feet
trailing behind,

your deep chest and slow beat
on the dazzling sky,
the house roofs defining
your passage which was silent
and so big and so brief
that I might as well have seen
a giraffe up there,
shone by the low winter sun.

It is this queer feeling
of not happening to look up
and it happening anyway
without our ever knowing.
Seeing the heron
was seeing
the knowing that it happens
whether we see it or not.

Song

So, here comes Winter, crying her power and her glory,
mocking at flesh, choosing bones for her bridal sheaf;

Bones, and the old bell-sounds of the stag, Hunger,
roaming about in the hills. Winter

that thins out the light and thickens the dark
and stills the running sound of water. Winter

that's broken only and over and over
by the dark speck, Seed, lodged in her womb.

Foxwinter

(for Dennis O'Driscoll)

Black nights, small splintery stars,
and baiting rat traps at the the kitchen table.
Dan said use chocolate spread and peanut butter.
A thick gob on a strip of tied-on rasher.
They'll stay around to lick and spring the trap.

A dog fox in the field in shine of snow;
each morning, in the gap, a little closer.
A lithe red fire, alive with winter.
Then someone shot him and the flame was quenched –
charred hearth of bones in January's frozen mud.

≈

Again the earth grows tight and cold and ancient,
the year rots down to dark and sunless days.
There's scuffle of new rats inside the wood-shed,
a vixen prowling covers in the long field,
the traps in ready heap beside the door.

How hard life is, what strange relentless splendour,
this killing-trap of birth and time and death,
that quenches light and douses fires and only love escapes –
to saunter off, untouched by the sprung steel,
and lays its head down in the trap set by the heart.

Threnody for Seamus

I've taken a sick dog to the vet and we're waiting.
A man comes in, youngish, his face full of weather,
asking for syringes and milk powder –
brand names I don't know, stuff for lambs.
I sit soothing the dog, watch Fiona
get things off the shelves, fill brown paper bags,
then send him away, his arms full.
That man's asleep on his feet, I say.
She laughs. *It's the time of the year* –
February – thin and hard and sharpened with rain,
a few snowdrops up, sticking close to the ground,
the river run wild, drowning fences, pulling trees
down into itself, and for some reason I start thinking
about where my life's gone – how it's slipping through my fingers
like the little bright fish in the handful of water
I dip for in August when this same river
has shallows
and pooled light
and banks blowsy with meadowsweet and agrimony,
all tumbled and trailed down into the water,
and the swallows make glitters of light taking flies,
and swimsuits hang on farm washing lines,
and the young girls stroll their stuff in pairs,
and the old women sit in the doorways, their stockings
rolled into soft latex doughnuts around their ankles,
and the land breathes and eases and stretches –
Not the usual time of year to go dying.

Life's like the fish, just a wriggle of light
that slips through your fingers
and slides away off down the river,
in February or May or even August.
And it's colder here without you.
And Dennis, already gone –

Report

There are no cows in Healy's fields,
though they must have been there this morning,
the splatters of shit in the grass are so fresh.
There's a monstrous gathering up by Joe Ryan's.
Dogs and cattle and a tractor with its engine running.
Joe Ryan was a dealer, he's retired, but keeps his hand in.
The paths I've followed are still rank with the smell of beasts,
which you never get when they're left to graze in peace.
I don't know what's going on in any of the fields
in the sense of markets, or what needs moving, or when,
but I always know what stock's in what field
on account of needing somewhere to run the dogs.

All the fields round us grow grass,
no one has any other crop up here on the hillside.
You can stand and watch the grain-fields across the valley
turning reddish gold before harvest. Tom and Rory
were bringing cattle down the hill two days ago,
and Tom called would I block the side road with the dogs.
He said they were a bit wild. Then he said to tell me the truth
they weren't far off – and he drew his hand across his throat
and I knew he meant the slaughter-house.
He didn't want to say it out in front of them, the same way
you wouldn't say in front of a child that his Mam hadn't long to live.
There are sheep in Pat's fields. They're all bones and angles
and such a clean white. They're not long after shearing.
They nose in thistles that are tall and close to bursting.

I know what's in the fields when it comes to wild flowers
and trees and what grows where. There's yarrow in the pastures now,
the blackberries are ripening. The crab-apple by the big old stones
looks like the tree did the winter we bought one too small
and everything in the Christmas box got crammed onto its branches.

The figwort is making tall spires of seed-heads, there's a black patch
in the grass by Healy's gate where someone's burned out a wasp's nest.

The swallows are flittering all over the place,
it won't be too long before they start lining the wires,
then one day we'll wake to bare skies. That's the real sign.
No matter what flowers late or how warm the days are,
it means the year's over, we won't see them back
till we've lived through another winter. We start looking out in April,
and sometimes they're a week early and sometimes they're late
but they come. One year I thought the winter had won.
I was walking the dogs by the river.
A short, bitter flurry of snow came blowing up over the water,
but in among the snow there were swallows and swifts.
I was telling this to a man in a bar one night. He asked what I felt
and I said I cried and he looked at me but he didn't say anything,
and I was glad I hadn't pretended or acted cool.

Lost Worlds

We played the footsteps game – I always won.
I would have cheated but I didn't need to.
I saw the space remember what had ceased.

When you were Grandmother, I won again.
I was as snail-slime, hardly moving.
You never sent me back, you couldn't cheat.

You were my childhood's deep companion –
the bright cry on the afternoon's green hill,
the broken water where we made our crossing.

The morning games – long faded, gone the meadow,
a lone hill sweeps its silent arc against the sky.
Those stepping stones are sunk too deep to tread.

The Latvians Stir Ghosts

When I saw her in her urban kitchen –
thin and smart in her charity-shop green dress –
a glass wall was between us
polished spotless with some soft cloth of mistrust.
All winter she'd lived up the hill
in the grey house with the damp walls,
the rains fading the fields. Then snow –
its ice-floe memories of Riga, darkness, home.

The nights we'd laboured at her table –
those filled-in forms, the dictionary, the child's first homework.
Together, sounding out the words
that marched beside the pictures in his school-book.
The dog, dancing the leatherette sofa.
The baby, heaving herself slowly upright.
The bitter, amber taste of milkless tea.
All those months of friendship and now nothing.

Was her warmth just a trick of survival
the child of an orphanage cannot unlearn?
Had my impulse been only my training
that no one should be so alone?
The house was old – others had strained before them
to keep the turf stacked and the children fed.
Awakening, had they heard that voiceless language
and lent us grace to mine a simpler truth?

Shame

No matter how you try, it won't refold,
smooth out or soften down to put away
into some drawer that's quietly pushed closed,
hiding the sound and fury of the day.

It is the sucking-rag of all your nights,
the childhood comforter gone strangely wrong,
the cloth you take to bed that breaks the heart,
the lullaby that morphs into a darker song.

Latvia Phones Ireland

(for Rimma Bulanova)

It is November.
I am making dinner when the phone rings.
Can you talk?
I switch off all the gas.

She is leaving Wolverhampton.
Tomorrow she will get a bus,
spread out her night things on some cousin's sofa,
in the morning, find a job, a room.

If I keep on saving
I can bring children here by Christmas.
Yes, yes, my health okay. My head not broken like in Ireland.
Children okay too. It is only that they are so far away.
She cries a little and I listen to her grief.
We speak of when she lived here, before England.
I meet you on the road. You tell me you are neighbour.
I go home, say to husband, what is neighbour?
We laugh.
She says she loves me then she ends the call.

I sit not noticing the dinner cooling.
Love and *neighbour* and a line gone dead.
How can she flick a gift like that
across the night from bedsit-Wolverhampton?
It is a boning knife that finds its home.

Night Journeys

We leave in the darkness,
cross over the mountains.
Small, silent villages
crouch in dawn's thinnings.

Black-boned trees gibbet
the spread skies of morning.
Lights bloom in upper rooms,
buildings swim clear.

Some secret is folded
away with night's cloth.
Starched high-feast linen
closed shut in a drawer.

Empires

(for Michael Longley)

Today our schedule says the Summer Palace.
After the glittering high-rise of Beijing,
I like its lowness in the damp, green light.

I stand to watch an old man tread the path –
he holds a pot of water; with a soft, long-handled brush,
forms characters that blossom black on slate,

then drying, disappear into the stone.
The translator – impatient – shoos me on;
she says his words don't matter, we must climb,

straight to the hill pagoda where the Golden Buddha waits,
his arms eternally arranged to bless.
There isn't any power in Buddha blessings.

I like the glow they make around the heart.
She has inherited the revolution,
holds her own future in her small, deft hands.

Below, the old man walks the granite path,
the water of his brush-strokes looms and fades,
his characters, their sensual, ancient forms,

glide back into the silence of the stone.

Dying

(i.m. David MacLennan 1948–2014)

Sooner or later
– because the way is always open –
sooner or later you will agree the invitation.

Then you'll be there, not here –
no longer hesitating in the doorless doorway,
but safe inside the dazzling dark, beyond the light.

Burying Barrie Cooke's Coffin

(March 2014)

We'd waked him, then painted his cardboard coffin.
In sun and in wind, we'd lowered it into the ground.
We'd stood around making long speeches, but he hadn't heard.
He'd been boxed far too long for a weight of fresh sods
to fasten him under the earth.

The Holiday

Look, we have made this.
Fragments of flowers and grasses and driftwood
scattered beside the salt sea.

It is so accidental.
These pieces of light laid flat on the tiles,
a striped dress that dries on a rail.

And so fragile.
The sound of the dishes he's moving around
in a kitchen that isn't ours.

Everything floats in the sun and the wind
and the tide slipping over the sands.
We will leave it to play, like a child we've set down

with a bucket and spade in the sun.
No one will ever return.
Photographs bleach into light.

Europe

It is seven o'clock on a beach in Cantabria.
The light is blueing, the tide
is on the way in.
Families pack to go home.
Sunshades close like bright flowers.
Children trot after trudging figures,
burdened with bags and with back-packs,
with armfuls of random possessions.
Some encampments
stay camped on the sands.
The light is changing.
I am reading a book
about Germany in the late thirties.
I look up.
Everyone seems sadder and more beautiful.

Return

(Northern Spain)

This is the room that we asked for,
its faded walls peaceful and shabby,
the dark polished boards of the floor.

I think someone died in this room,
emptied the self of itself,
to leave something sunlit and quiet,

a queer, tired stillness and peace.
I wake in it after an absence
in which I have had to lean closer,

ear pressed to invisible walls.
Something has moved to the light,
though all seems just as it was –

street sounds and sun and bright voices,
balcony windows half open,
stirrings that call from below.

The Pilgrim's Warning

Do not fall sick in Santiago.
Regard the all-but-windowless walls
of the Hospital San Roc
and refrain from contracting more ailments
than those you had when you came here.
If you are hunchback or brokeback or cripple
go straight to the great Cathedral.
Miraculous and infallible,
Sant Iago will certainly heal you.
Do not run with bad company
after your cure. The chances are you'll fall ill
with a plague or a desperate ague.
The Hospital of San Roc
is enormous and forbidding.
You'll lie on a heap of stale straw,
or peer through the high, shuttered windows,
and nothing to see but stone roof-tops,
nothing that grows or decays,
that is warm or alive or fallible.

Two Funerals

(for Bairbre and Marian Lonergan)

They were as green
as freshly gathered herbs, already wilting.
Too close together.
Everyone asked, but no answer.
Everyone felt their life suffer.
The hardship. Behind me someone said
this sort of thing should be against the law.

Countrymen

(for Jim Barcoe)

We were sitting in the Abbey, waiting,
and he was telling me, low-voiced,
about their week-old spaniel pups,
the one with the tail that was two-thirds brown,
white only up near the tip.

If he cut for the flash
she'd be like the mother,
tail over-long,
and ribboned
by furze and briar.
Ah, to hell with the theory,
the theory and the purists.
Blaze or no blaze, he'd cut her short.
He'd not see her hurt, like Jess.

It was November,
the old year was slipping, the new
drawing closer.
There were monks drifting through,
pressed close to the walls
and in the worn places –
drawn back to mark
these eight hundred years
the Cistercians had lived in the valley.

He would do it himself?

He would. A hot knife. Fast. Heat sealing
the cut flesh. His hands mimed
the knife and the pup. I watched them –
the swift, sure cut,

against the dark wood – the monks crowded in
for a better look.
                    I thought of our pups.
Warm flesh-sacks. How they'd jumped in my hands
as the clippers closed. And the small bloody heap
on the vet's table. The monks were remembering
the oddness of hands, smells, blood, you could feel them
growing focused, thickening, remembering
the body's red roar
                    from a past stretching back
till it slid off the edge
of time and the world,
and a dog and a man –
through first light,
through last light – a man and a dog
moving always together.

Reflection

There's a line of light on the lake through the sieving rain,
and swallows, skimming the face of the rushy meadow.
A grid of stone walls, loosening, falling away.

The terrain external mirrors the terrain internal.
Swallows, skimming the face of the rushy meadow.
Thoughts, breaking the line of the line of light.

The Conjurer

(for Campbell McGrath)

I met this American, sprung like those clips on a clip-frame,
the ones that fly off, the moment you get the image you've
chosen more or less aligned with glass and backing.

I've just done just that. The clips have flown and I've
crawled around on the floor, bottom up, like Heaney's skunk,
trying to find the bits that have gone missing.

I find the clip. I straighten up and swipe at the dust
balls that hang from my jeans like bees that are thinking of
swarming. I wriggle the metal bit over the glass and press
the clip home. It's a postcard of Bosch's Conjurer. On the
back it says the original lives in St Germain-en-Laye.

I should like to go to the Musée in St Germain-en-Laye.
In the painting a man in rose-red with a venal face is doing
some trick moving cups and balls around on a wooden
table. There's an egg-basket hooked at his waist. A barn
owl is poking its halved head out, looking tightly into some
distance of feather and claw. Opposite, at the front of the
crowd, the fool bends over the table. A fat purse hangs
from his belt. His mouth is open and his jaw has dropped.
He's trying to outwit the showman, to figure out the trick
he knows is being played. Another man stands behind the
fool, his hand on his victim's purse.

Where was I? Back with that American. Wound up so
tight in summer Dublin that I couldn't work him out. When
he went home to the States he sent me his poems and I
opened a smooth-faced book that I didn't want. I was tired
of poems – their carefulness, their form and rhyme and
crafted double meanings.

But I read, and a pile of gold coins shone from the pages,
a stack of brightness that teetered a moment then spilled
out onto my table. And I was the drop-jawed fool who

watched as the showman moved things around and lifted a cup I could have sworn was empty. His accomplice silently stole my purse, his owl peered out of the wicker basket strapped to the belt at his waist.

Caherdaniel

It is morning again in our holiday house on a back-strand
that brims with the tide like a dinner plate left in the rain.

Each day I stand within its circle of attention.
The water gleams and glimmers at my feet.

I wander off to poke its patterned edges–
fringed rushes, quiet gull-talk, feathers, prints.

The Sea and Seashore book that's in my back-pack,
is left there while I leave myself and wait

until the urge for ordering has left me,
and emptiness runs in a tide across my sands.

Atlantic Island

This island's a hard-time woman. Squally and bitter and always more weather, blowing straight in from the sea. Sometimes she sits at the stained wooden table, stares at her nicotined fingers and weeps. Sea wrack lies out on her beaches. The stormy light gleams on her sands. Gulls wheel and jeer, doors bang and blow, her long waves are running for cover. Sometimes she's taken by longing. She opens her legs in the night. How her waters are black, how their depths lap the rocks, how they shine where the moon's riding high.

Then she's tossing out boats to the sharks. There's a dull, heavy look in her eyes. Planks swash around, torn anchor-buoys bob, a life-jacket's snarled in the weed. She smashes the neck of the bottle. Drinks deep from its jagged green throat. Her dark hair swings lank round the bones of her shoulders, her long hissing waves break and foam.

Poplars

He planted poplars
too bare and graceful for that lumpy hillside.
In winter she'd no shelter
from wind or their only neighbours,
their windows inching closer.

But spring came and the poplars
swayed in the sweeter wind like temple dancers.
She saw that he could wait
for a place in his life where the light turned
leaves into running water.

November

Old gods
creep the bare earth.
Old sun
seeps over its rim.

Sheep cough,
limp fading grass.
Mud-prints in gaps
fill and glaze over.

Only the crows,
playing catch-as-catch-can,
tumble and rise.
The light dies.

Late Thoughts

I think my perinatal bone's re-opening
and I have whizzed out through the soft hole in my head.
I have such thoughts – the doors have all flown wide –
the furniture's outside, it shines with rain.

Is this what growing old is really all to do with,
this flying through the air and turning inside out?
I thought I was a house with beds and tables,
with dining-chairs and clocks and parquet floors.

Did I convince myself I needed all this clutter?
What made me think I'll end up somehow wiser
than if I'd just invited in bright spirits
and left my doors wide open to the sky?

Software Update

Skullcap, mullein,
fleabane, clover,

horehound, borage,
lesser lousewort –

shrivelled stalks
of arcane language,

fallen out of
broke-backed book-spine,

lost, all lost,
words, wild and sunlit,

wind and sod
and blowing light.

The New Widow

(for Mary Doyle)

Her husband has died in the night.
The first neighbours are gathering.

Someone has set on the table
a baby, asleep in a rocker.

Someone else hoovers the front room.
The kettle is on for more tea.

The widow – not young, not old –
is asked what she needs from the shop.

She stares, shakes her head.
What would she want from a shop?

The baby awakens and gurgles.
She stubs out her cigarette.

The dogs stir, they're old;
knowing nothing of babies,

they snuffle and stalk the strange sounds.
One of them growls

then they settle.
This is a first for them all.

How It Happens

Yesterday someone up there in the sky
threw down a bucket
of mist and green mud,
and the spring spilled out
in a wash of bright rain
and broken light, coming and going.

Away from Home

It is hot and still. A jay
is gulping the food set out for the cat
from a dish on the stones by the pond.
He knows I'm here but he's turned his back
so he won't have to tend to his fear.

Just the same
he eats fearfully. The air
is blank and thick with heat.
A glass vase on the table
holds the same blue as the jay.

Suddenly,
as I have never understood before,
I understand heat in mid-afternoon.
The way it holds all life in stillness.
In silence and the sameness of the light.

I understand that I am far from home,
where jays are rarely sighted, where the day
scurries and blows across the wayward skies.
I understand that life is warm and fickle,
that nothing holds, that I no longer know,
and California is a merciless concept.

Erika

California was boring.
All those gold-grass hills and redwoods.
Not intimate or nestled at the heart.
The light was too unvaried.
The ocean too majestic.
The roads were wide, the cars were big,
the stores were full of wonders.

When I gave this verdict
to a German artist
she threw back
her tangled head and laughed.

Very good, she said.
California. Boring.
I think that's what I'll tell them in Berlin.

We were sitting on a beach beside an inlet.
Her legs were stretched out,
sturdy, brown and strong.
She laughed again, reached for another sandwich,
and all the time she watched two Californians,
arms held out to either side for balance,
wading very slowly out to sea.

Both were thin and in their early seventies.
The gleam of water touched their neat black swimsuits.
What astonished was the curious shyness
of those wistful, stretching-out white hands.

I think I'll make a film when I go home.
Just three minutes. Showing only hands.
Call it
How to Love People.

At the Musée Cluny

The Kings of Judah,
their gouged noses, broken faces.
The Kings of Judah,
their pocked cheeks and eyeless gazes.

The Kings of Judah,
their great heads, their shattered crowns.
The Kings of Judah,
they look on –

Above, upon a broken slab,
a woman presses in behind a monk,
her smile lascivious
as the Wife of Bath.

There are no kings of Judah now,
and all the lyres have come unstrung
and all the boundaries are undrawn
but antique lechery lives on.

PART TWO

The essay and the sequence of poems that follow were written after the death in Delhi, India, of my youngest brother, Paddy Jolley, in January 2012. Paddy was a photographer and a filmmaker. He was working on a version of *Finnegans Wake* at the time of his death from a heart attack at the age of just 47. His partner, Lu Thornely and their two young sons, Ned and Thomas, had been staying with her cousin and his family in Sri Lanka. Paddy was cremated in Delhi in accordance with Hindu funeral rites.

The essay is a meditation on grief and is not specific to my brother's death.

All the poems except the first one are addressed to him personally. They are really one long poem, but they are separated out to help the reader to understand the events behind them. They are dedicated to Lu and their children, who have helped to fill the empty space left by Paddy's death.

Aftermath

Two summers ago we spent a couple of weeks in a cottage on the Iveragh Peninsula in County Kerry. For the first week the rain was relentless. Out on the side of a mountain with two young spaniels who needed exercise, I lost my footing in driving rain and fell into a bog hole. Flailing around in the half light in water up to my chest, I made contact with something bubbling and putrid and mostly submerged. I was sharing the bog hole with the rotting remnants of a long dead sheep.

Unlike the sheep I managed to crawl from the hole, then stumbled back down the mountain into a steaming hot bath. My clothes went into the washing machine, came out, went in. Again and again and again. There'd been a scummy slick on the bog water, a skim of greyish bubbles and strands of old wool. It must have been the oils from the animal's body. Now I couldn't get the death-smell out of my clothes, now matter how often I washed them. Nor out of my skin though I scrubbed it with sweet-smelling soap.

I became obsessively conscious of it. I would sit at my table in the rented house, unable to work. There were spreading brown stains on the plastered wall beside me that came from the heat of the huge old chimney-flue behind the wall. I imagined the warmth of the room was increasing the smell and drawing it from my skin. I moved downstairs but it was no better.

A few days later we went to a friend's for dinner, a house on the edge of the sea. I sat in a room full of books and talk and food, a life far removed from the bog and moor and silence of the mountains. Self-conscious, I put my arm behind my back, but an arm is attached to the body and can't be altogether dispensed with. The smell came slinking out into the room and licked itself round me. Convinced that it was rank and authentic, I began to explain to the woman I was talking to. She said she had a wonderful nose and demanded a sniff at my arm. I held it out.

'Imagination,' she pronounced decisively.

I thought at the time that it must have been a neurotic reaction.

I have since been surprised at the number of people who confirmed the experience and spoke of a similar obsession with smell following contact with something dead.

Perhaps, like death itself, the smell stays in the nostrils long after the actual occasion has passed. Perhaps the body holds onto the smell of another body's demise, even if the body isn't human. Worse if it's human: war diaries all record being overwhelmed by smell. Presumably it's the shock of premonition: the recognition by the body of its own mortality, its terror at the unavoidable abandonment that is coming to it.

A young woman whose father was killed in a car crash told me of her inability to manage her life for a long time after the event. As well as the grief that overwhelmed her in the immediate aftermath, she described its unpredictable reappearance in the most unlikely times and situations. She also spoke of making stupid mistakes, of confusion in managing the simplest transactions, of losing words in company.

She said that fifty years ago she'd have slipped a black armband onto her sleeve every morning for a year before she left the house. She talked of how, in modern Celtic-Tiger Ireland, she had longed for an armband because it would have explained her situation, have been like the red light flashing on the car that drives ahead of a vehicle that's too long or too wide or too slow for the road that it's travelling.

Look out. Here come's grief.

Everyone stops or pulls into the side and makes allowances.

That's completely gone now. We still do the death-thing – the wake, the vigil, the removal and the funeral. It's very communal, very intense. But when all that's done we get up in the morning thinking that somehow it's over. We expect ourselves to be able to act as though this event that blocked out the stars has safely moved into the past. We are unprepared for the sheer intensity of the pain that's about to kick in.

But the death-smell is in our nostrils and in our clothes and deep in the pores of our skin. Though strangers cannot smell it, we can smell nothing else.

When death happens we find that a part of us already knows quite a lot about the corporeal side of what has to be coped with. We may not have fought in a war or worked in an abattoir or fallen into a bog-hole with a dead sheep, but we've all experienced the private reality of our own physicality, we know about blood and pain and shit and our own fear of it. We are generally less overwhelmed by the sight of death than we think we will be.

What is so surprising is that we have supposed that seeing the corpse is the greater part of what we will have to deal with.

The suffering that we experience at the death of someone we love very much – especially when that death is untimely and we feel that a life has not been lived – is unimaginably painful. What is even more shocking is that there is nothing that can be done to relieve this pain, we just have to trudge through each day and endure it. Sometimes we think we can't.

Everyone tells us this pain will lessen but they speak from a reality that has very little to do with us, even if they have themselves experienced what we are now going through. So it isn't that we don't believe them: we simply stare at them blankly waiting for their mouths to stop moving.

That they are speaking from a different reality is literally true. Death pushes us deeper into our lives, we act and react from a place that is not normally accessible to us, we experience phenomena that at other times we would be unable to experience. Where does the spirit go when it leaves the body behind it? I don't know, but I think there is an intermediate stage when it still has occasional access to the life it previously occupied, however briefly. Immediately following an important death there is the possibility of an inter-change that would not otherwise happen and that mostly disappears once we have moved back into our normal lives and the dead have moved on to other realms. This can be both comforting and disturbing. With the passing of time it happens less frequently and is less intense. Both parties are moving away from each other and are becoming established in their changed state of being. Slowly the suffering of he (or she) who loves lessens until the day comes when there are moments when it is almost absent. If these moments join up for even a brief period of time, then we are capable of relaxing into a state of non-suffering. Once non-suffering becomes established there is again the possibility of joy. (Strangely it is possible to experience joy when in a state of physical suffering, but emotional suffering cancels it out.)

The return of joy, however fleeting, is usually accompanied by feelings of betrayal and hence the return of suffering. A yo-yo movement has begun. There is a gap in the intensity of our grief so life rushes in. Fear of the return of intense suffering is almost as painful as the suffering itself.

People talk a lot about anger following a death, but perhaps this anger is simply a variation on suffering – a kind of substitute that happens when the truly devastating pain has eased for a little and it is possible to be angry at the person who has died for causing it. If the relationship was complicated and there were a lot of unresolved issues then the feeling of abandonment that has caused the anger is more intense. There are also the bubbles of gas that rise up from the body in the bog-hole. Sometimes we discover things we did not know, are brought face to face with aspects of the dead person they have concealed from us. It doesn't have to be the mistress who turns up at the funeral. There are often small ambushes, many of them simply things we chose not to see.

The emotional instability around anger, betrayal and pain bring us close to chaos. But a return to "normality" would mean an odd kind of loss. Somewhere there is an awareness in us that we are living on a different plane, and somewhere we also crave the purity and intensity of this plane – as those whose lungs are used to high clean air crave relief from the smog and fumes of a city. On this other level it is possible to be alone with your dead and to feel their presence. This is hard to let go of, though it must be accomplished. It is the only thing that will bring about the release of the dead. To dwell there too long is not our purpose in life. Somehow we must find the grace to accept the living.

I think we are "saved" back into life by matter. The weeks and months pass and the flesh we inhabit reasserts its dominance. The weight returns to the things of the world and the strange clear light that we lived in becomes too strange and clear. The disturbing feelings of guilt at the prospect of a return to a state of being that is closer to normality begin to recede. We want food, warmth, density. The wet dogs drying in the heat of a fire that is contained and domesticated, its ferocious energy channeled through a hearth and a chimney.

But we have experienced that energy, and the plaster on our wall is discoloured and disfigured like the flue-wall in that cottage in the mountains. We know its power. Every time the phone rings our equanimity is shattered – we are back in the bog-hole, floundering around in disaster. And the reality of our existing disaster makes the potential for further disaster unlimited. We have lost all trust in dailiness. No amount of reassurance can counter the continuing psychic disturbance our dreams convey to us. All is not right. It will never be right in quite the same way again. We have made contact with what is deep inside us and also with what is beyond us. There is a pathway opened between them.

It is important to remember that the dead do not belong to us. When a death is that of a young child it is all but impossible to grasp this. A young child is dependent and in our care. When they die we feel that our roles continue. This is also true of adults where the parents and siblings have had a strong nurturing role. They know they must cede this role to the wife, husband or partner, in death as in life, but the weight of years makes that harder to do. There are so many photographs and memories that happened before the new union. In death, the first family yearns to reclaim its child. The partner is also staking a claim. Everything gets confused. Hence the unseemly scramble for possessions after a death.

Obtaining a possession is like proof of ownership. Possessions are valuable, not for themselves, but for their relationship to the person who has died. A lighter, a wallet, a hairbrush – intimate things that were used every day – become charged. We imagine they retain something of their owner. By treasuring them we think we can somehow prolong their belonging among us.

But the dead belong to themselves. They have completed their lives, even if the death came about through violence. Somewhere a contract has been signed off on and nothing will undo what has been done. Nor can we follow them or hold onto them once they have ceased to meet with us on the plane of between. We can only cherish what we have experienced and let go.

What's Left

(for Lu)

I do not move much beyond matter.
What is touched, seen, heard.

The stunned bird kicks in my hand.
I watch its eyes dull and glaze over.
It is mute, warm, dead.

I trust in its death.
That it lived, that it died.
Stay. Hold out your hand.
your fingers linked his.
My hand seeks yours.
This is the chain of belonging.
This is as much as I know.

After You Died

I am in Dunnes Stores
thumbing through a rack of wet-suits
trying to find an age-4 for your son.

You are in a rented room in Delhi
smoking and making notes for your latest film.

These days
I am always stuck in Dunnes Stores
trying to find the right wet-suit.
You are always alone in a narrow room,
smoking and making notes.
Your heart is failing but you still don't know it.
It's hard to breathe – for me, as well as for you.
Sometimes I wish I could stop loving you.

≈

I am sitting up in bed in the rented house.
The cover is black and white stripes.
There are two windows to the room.
In front of me lies the inlet
and a big lump of raw-boned hillside
crowned with soft soggy cloud.
The window beside the bed
frames sky and thin-coloured sands
woven with marram grass.
I am thinking of the drawer I opened in my mother's study,
the hundreds of your photos that I found there
from that first India trip.

≈

I dipped Thomas into the waves.
He liked being dipped,
he slapped at the water and splashed.
He's one year old and one month.
You've been dead for just seven months.
When I was fifteen I dipped you into the waves.

≈

When I saw the Sidney Nolan picture
of Ned Kelly's sister quilting his black helmet
I knew that's what I'd always tried to do.
A useless love-filled gesture,
the failure of the gesture,
the blood on the blue quilting,
the blood on your face in the morgue.

≈

If it hadn't been India
it would have been somewhere else.
Perhaps I'm glad it was India.
Perhaps I'm glad that your window
opened onto the market.
And over the road, the pigeons,
soft coloured rows in their boxes,
talking in low tumbling voices
lost in the roar from the street.

≈

Had you already drowned in India?
There was the photo of the Ganges,
the liquid light floating the evening water,
the way you broke it as you raised your hand to wave,
the time that you went swimming from the ghats.

Your Box

They put your ashes in a wooden box. It was a handsome box with a lock and two keys, and ornamental metal chasing round the base and the lid. I carried you through security, Séan carried your three-year-old, Lu carried your baby. In the plane, we put you in the overhead luggage bins with all the other hand-baggage. It was a long journey. The baby was in one of those fold-down cribs, but the stewardess wouldn't let your three-year-old sleep on the floor. I wouldn't let her wake him. I told her you'd just died. I said the plane wasn't full, there was plenty of room in the next section – if we couldn't leave the child on the floor she could move one of the people lying stretched across three seats. She went away. She came back. Lu carried him through and laid him down, still sleeping, across two cleared seats. I sat beside him while he slept.

When we got to London Lu's father was waiting. They took your bags and we took your box. We went to a Pret A Manger to buy a sandwich before the Dublin flight. Séan was at the counter paying. You were heavy so I put you on the floor. Two young Australian lads standing beside me noticed your box and began to admire it. They asked where I'd got it? I said it was my brother's ashes, I was taking them home to Ireland. I think they thought they hadn't heard right. Then they looked at each other's faces and they knew they had. They said they were sorry. Then they weren't there, and Séan was handing me a camembert and cranberry sandwich in a cardboard wrapper.

Watching the Fire Take Your Body

Remember those blue irises I'd left for years?

You dug them out with Séan's big fork,
then left them on the grass for me to split.

After you'd gone I wrenched and tore.
Got nowhere, gave up struggling, fetched the spade.

That mat of yellow roots, the slicing blade,
the last despairing heave, the rain of soil –

the shock still live and scorching through my flesh.

The Door

Suddenly there was a different significance in everything. Sometimes I disappeared from myself. Everything stilled, I'd be watching a bird pecking around on the gravel and yet there was no one inside me to watch. I would look around the room I was in, but no one inside me was looking. I lost all concept of time passing. Fear didn't exist. Then gradually the world would begin to re-form into a more familiar state.

After such an experience I would be confused and tired and dissatisfied. I would go for long walks and reorganise the flower garden, moving the plants from where they'd always lived to somewhere else. At first I thought I might be dying myself, I thought that perhaps I had a brain tumour. Once or twice I almost said it to Séan but the words didn't come. Once out, there'd be doctors and tests, and the possibility of treatment. Sometimes I saw Séan look at me then look quickly away. So he, too, had decided to say nothing.

Then I began to realise that something different was going on, that the stillness came from a different level. When there was *no one there*, I hadn't left myself, it was only that my 'I' had been dissolved into something wider.

And I understood afresh that everyone is always inside the act of dying at the same time as being inside the act of living. The door is always open, and there'd been no choice for you anymore than there'd be choice for me if I had a fatal and inoperable brain tumour. You'd simply walked through the door that you'd stood beside since the day of your birth.

Life Gone Away Is Called Death.

This couple that we met who live in Dresden
sent us a book of photos of their city,
all taken when the war was near its end.

Sometimes the dead are sitting in the rubble
still warmly dressed in coats and hats and boots,
their shoulders resting casually together,

companionable, despite the strangeness,
the hollowing eyes, the skim of wrinkled milk,
the frame of bone just working to the surface.

I don't know why we need to live in bodies,
or why, when we have left, they hang around,
still stubbornly at home in linear time.

Fragment

I'm reading the book you lent Séan
a few weeks before you died.
Some of the pages have their corners folded over.

I'm flickering through the book,
grubbing for more turn-downs,
scanning the text beneath to guess your mind –

Why can't I leave you alone and stop prying?
What is it that I need to understand?

Child

When you'd been dead a year he found the bag –
those clothes you'd worn in India – not unpacked.

He tucked them round the edges of his bed.
Lu saw, said nothing, let him take his time.

After a while he put them back himself. His body
must have drawn from yours the strength it needed.

Thirteen Months

When the bus from Dublin drew in
I didn't see your long stretch
swing down through the opened door.

There was only the calling of crows
high in the empty trees,
only the morning light on the winter grass.

So it seems I don't have to lose you over and over,
each time a Kavanagh's bus
pulls in off the Carlow Road.

It makes me feel weightless and plundered.
You're walking off into the distance,
you don't want us pulling you back.

In San Vicente

Hiddenness is the ballast on the ship's keel, the great underwater portion of a life that steadies the rest.

JANE HIRSHFIELD

The morning is sunlit and still. It is like being inside the shell of an oyster. There is light gleaming on the edge of the table and on the side of the closed book. It is coming in low from the East.

The sorrow says 'of what use are such observations? That which may be called joy, and which may, in time, return, will not be making observations.'

So sorrow must be to do with not being at the centre, with being only partially present in life. Sorrow wants to live in a photograph or in a memory.

Yesterday it was raining so we went to the great, disused church on the hill. When I went into the church I was looking for something hidden. I found nothing. There was a vast stone nave, a carved and painted altarpiece, some side chapels.

Jane Hirshfield is a Buddhist. Buddhists are into the wisdom of hiddenness. When we came out of the church there was daylight. There were people, wandering about in the rain. I think hiddenness is all around us. If by hiddenness you mean what is precious and mysterious. It is very simple and very visible and flourishes best when it isn't organised. Like Joy.

Empty Space Poem, Eighteen Months

In the photo there's a child astride your shoulders.
You are moving through the cut-gold of a field.

The hedgerow trees are thickening and darkening.
The sky's a constant, clear, heraldic blue.

You are on the right side, walking slowly.
The left side of the meadow's deep and still.

I've cut it down the middle, framed and hung it.
We pass you every time we climb the stairs.

Which leaves the empty half for me to deal with:
the empty field, the hedgerow-trees, the sky.

I've framed that too, I keep it on the shelf
above my desk, slipped in between two books.

I tell myself you're everywhere around me.
That summer is still sumptuous, people die.

These are the separated halves of the same picture.

Company

We two went swimming very early. A fine mist
billowed on the still green lake and shrouded the far trees.

We toweled off in the silence, hardly speaking.
A heron moved its station in the shallows.

There's no one else who would have done this with me:
swum so far out, and at that hour, and into such deep water.

Strange how your absence
can allow your presence.

Between Here and There

It is so still your heart would break with longing:
watching the world awaken from the mild, calm night.

A brown hare lopes across dew-thickened grass,
the deep woods yield and open to receive it.

I'm drawn now to all frontiers, shadows, borders,
edges of fields and roads and open places,

where space runs out of being space and changes
into a refuge from the weight of being seen.

Moving On

The morning – sullen,
a dull cloth.

Frog-spawn in the ditches
thickens like thought.

Some shoulder's pushing
against an unlatched door.

Nothing beyond
but empty, whitening air.

Already it's too late
for winter's splintered light,

its rank folds, thorned weave,
its clean, bitter stars.

The levels change, a subtle shift
it takes a while to grasp.

Suns

Alive we are autistic, stuck in detail.
It is a necessary way to be.

Don't mind the dead bees, sweep them from the table.
Their sting's long gone, the thread that strung them, broken.

Your pyre is ash, it floats the wind, remember and forget.
So many suns we made of honey.

NOTES

Vacances (19) is a response to a small painting by Bonnard that hangs in the National Gallery, Dublin.

Nobby of the Bogs (20) is a traditional name for a grey heron. In some parts it is Jenny of the Bogs.

Empires (31). I wrote this poem after hearing Barry Guy improvising with Agustí Fernández and Ramón López. I never discovered what the old man in the poem was writing, but I knew the incident was important as well as poignant, though I didn't then understand why. When I heard the performance, it occurred to me that "impermanence" can outlast empires, both material and spiritual – that a sound vibrating into silence, a brush-stroke disappearing into stone, have a resonance that is more ancient than the organisation of societies. It is dedicated to Michael Longley because his work can have the same quality.

Countrymen (39). Traditionally hunting dogs have their tails cut short so they won't be damaged when working heavy cover. The cut is usually made at the point of the 'flash' or white marking, even if this leaves it over-long. 'The Abbey' is the 13th-century Cistercian Abbey in Graiguenemanagh, Co. Kilkenny.

At the Musée Cluny (54). The 13th-century statues of the Kings of Judah which once graced the front facade of Notre Dame were torn down during the French Revolution. They have been replaced with replicas. Those recovered from their place of burial and are now in the Musée Cluny.

Suns (78). The quotation comes from Poem 116 by Osip Mandelstam, translated by Clarence Brown and W.S. Merwin.